THE joy OF living WITH less

THE joy OF living WITH less

HOW TO DOWNSIZE TO 100 ITEMS AND LIBERATE YOUR LIFE

mary lambert

CICO BOOKS
LONDON NEW YORK

Published in 2020 by CICO Books
An imprint of Ryland Peters & Small Ltd
20–21 Jockey's Fields   341 E 116th St
London WC1R 4BW   New York, NY 10029

www.rylandpeters.com

First published in 2013 as *Living with Less*

10 9 8 7 6 5 4 3 2 1

A CIP catalog record for this book is available
from the Library of Congress and the British
Library.

ISBN: 978 1 78249 822 3

Printed in China

Editor: Marion Paull
In-house editor: Dawn Bates
In-house designer: Eliana Holder
Art director: Sally Powell
Production controller: Mai-Ling Collyer
Publishing manager: Penny Craig
Publisher: Cindy Richards

CONTENTS

introduction

Having spent over 20 years helping clients to declutter their homes, I've witnessed close up how truly liberating and fulfilling the process can be. The people I've worked with have often become defined and weighed down by their many possessions. Once they are surrounded by fewer items, and have a more pleasurable and ordered living space, they find an inner spiritual contentment that enhances both their physical and emotional wellbeing.

Of course, the benefits of living with less go beyond the individual to the wider world. One of the many joys of buying less is the positive impact it has on the environment. Most goods have to be packaged, transported, and disposed of, and the more we buy, the more we contribute to this. If you choose to buy fewer things, you're likely to choose quality over throwaway items, leading to a reduced amount of waste. And, of course, once you have less you might even need less space, and that's good for the environment on so many levels.

I've written many books on decluttering, so in this one I wanted to set a new challenge: downsizing your personal possessions to just 100 items. I decided to take on the challenge myself as I wrote the book and you can follow my experiences in my personal journal throughout.

Get ready to feel overjoyed rather than overwhelmed by your possessions. Once you're living with less, you'll never look back.

THE 100-ITEM CHALLENGE

The challenge is to pare down your personal belongings to just 100 items (you can group some things together as one) and live with just these for a year. You can replace items but you can't add to your list, unless you have managed to keep it to fewer than 100 to begin with. This is a difficult goal to achieve, especially if you love new clothes, but it will change your attitude to buying forever. It will also make you realize how many things you have that you don't really need.

Clothes make up 70 percent of the 100-item challenge but do you realize that most of us wear only 20 percent of these? The rest just hang in the closet. Selling or giving away the ones that you don't wear, that don't fit, or that you don't like any more will make you much more conscious of the outfits that flatter you. And you will become adept at mixing and matching the clothes you have left.

To help you cope with the challenge, I have separated it into achievable goals that you can work on over a period of a year (or longer if you need it), so that you can find joy in the process rather than feel overburdened by it. The clothes goal is the biggest one, so it has the longest time allocated to it—4½ months. Others deal with fewer items, such as your electrical, electronic, and sports equipment, so these are given just 1½ months each. Releasing these possessions from your life may be hard at first but it will make you feel so free and give you extra energy to try new activities. Another benefit of letting go is that you can sell those things, or if you decide to donate some of your unwanted possessions to charity, instead, you will benefit from the "feel-good" factor of doing this.

ROOM-BY-ROOM DECLUTTERING

Just letting go of some of your personal possessions is not enough if you really want to live with less. You also need to appraise the household paraphernalia that you have accumulated over the years. If you look through each room in your home, you will notice how cluttered some areas have become, especially if you have been living there a while. Some rooms may be so full of furniture or equipment that you just don't use them any more. With my guidance you can allocate a certain number of hours to decluttering each room. Start on your worst room first, going through the main problem areas, using my solutions to help you restore some order to these over-loaded spaces.

A NEW LIFE

As the energy shifts and changes in your home, your own perspective will change as well. You will start to enjoy the clearer and more functional spaces in all your rooms. By clearing out, you will also allow "space" in your mind for new creativity.

Living with less helps you to find your true self beneath the clutter, and follow your heart's desires, which you may have neglected for a while. Time with family and friends will never seem so precious. But most of all, you can slow down and appreciate the wonders of your life, dreaming of all those unknown adventures that are yet to come.

PART 1

getting prepared

Getting into the right frame of mind to let go of possessions is hard to do, but once you start releasing them, the feel-good factor will soon set in and you will begin to feel liberated and fulfilled. The atmosphere in a home that is no longer cluttered will feel vibrant, and this will have the wonderful ripple effect of enhancing your overall wellbeing.

THE BENEFITS OF A SIMPLER LIFE

The rewards of living with less are truly amazing. You will find an inner spiritual contentment and joy that you just did not think was possible, and be happy in the knowledge that your actions will impact positively on those close to you and on the wider world.

- **Less time spent caring for possessions.** The more goods you have in your home, the more time you spend mending, cleaning, tidying, and maintaining them. This can leave you emotionally and physically drained, especially if you don't need the items, or even enjoy having them.

- **More kindness.** You will have more free time and energy, and extra money from buying less or selling possessions. You may decide to help others less privileged than yourself. Giving time or money to charities, or supporting good causes in the community, is far more satisfying than buying something new.

- **Less environmental impact.** Many goods are packaged in plastic, which takes years to degrade. By reducing the amount you buy, you are reducing the quantity of packaging you are responsible for, and also the number of discarded articles that will need recycling.

- **Less envy.** Today's media constantly show us celebrities at play, making us envious of their lavish lifestyles. By deciding to live with less you can reject wanting to live a more upmarket lifestyle.

- **Less need to keep up with modern trends.** You will reduce your desire to conform to the latest style, whether it be in fashion, decoration, or design.

- **More contentment.** A simpler lifestyle allows you time to follow your dreams. You may take up that hobby that you have never previously found time for, passionately pursue a new sport, or just spend more time with your family and friends.

hoarding TOO MANY possessions

Before you start your 100-item challenge and set off on the road to your minimalist lifestyle, you need to look at why you have acquired so many things in the first place.

I have come across many homes so full of possessions that the family could hardly move around them—and it doesn't stop there. I am often shown a garage or shed that is equally full, mainly with junk that has been stored and forgotten about. When I question my clients about why they have accumulated so many things, the answer is usually vague, along the lines of "it just sort of happened", or "I don't like to waste things." After some more gentle probing, I often discover that at least one family member can't stop buying, or one is a complete hoarder.

Hoarders will hold on to things they do not really want or need. They are just obsessed with the need to buy and accumulate. Sometimes these people are information addicts who feel compelled to save newspapers, magazines, or brochures, so that when they have time, they can read all the useful information they believe to be contained in them. And they do not just hoard new items. When a close relative dies, for example, rather than keeping the odd personal memento, they keep the majority of their relative's possessions, making their own home a mausoleum to someone else's past.

how hoarding possessions affects your home

As a feng shui consultant, I improve the energy flow in people's homes. According to the ancient Chinese practice of feng shui, an invisible life force—electro-magnetic meridians of energy called chi—flows through all things. It is important that this life force flows positively through your home to create a good atmosphere, but if your home is full of clutter or is overloaded with possessions, the flow is inhibited, and this creates a very lethargic and stale atmosphere.

Another tenet of feng shui is that we all have an inner/outer reality. So if your home is full of junk and has stale energy, it will have an effect on you both emotionally and spiritually, making you feel down and lacking direction and focus in your life. When you finally let go of unwanted belongings that have been stored in your home for years, it is really liberating and can be like a breath of fresh air or a major spring-clean. This, in turn, will have a huge effect on you, giving you new inspiration and a positive direction for your life.

WHY DO PEOPLE HOARD?

One of the major reasons is the feeling of security that hoarding brings. Some people become emotionally attached to the things around them. Looking at objects or other accessories that they have acquired over the years makes them feel happy and safe. Some even keep mementoes from unhappy events, refusing to remember the pain involved, or hang on to a gift that they dislike for fear of upsetting the person who gave it to them if they passed it on. Giving away or throwing out items they no longer need but to which they have an emotional attachment can be painful, tantamount to rejecting a friend's generosity.

different types of hoarders

When friends choose gifts, they do so with a loving intention, and these feelings can become bound up in the energy of the objects, which is why it can be so hard to let go of them. Sometimes true hoarders feel that part of their identity is attached to their possessions, and that by giving them away they are losing part of themselves.

Depression or grief can also fuel buying sprees, and when this comes on top of a compulsion to own the latest gadget, despite having many more at home, belongings can start piling up to an overwhelming extent, making it more difficult to shift them.

Creative people often save things to further their art and can easily become hoarders. Often they accumulate so many art supplies that they get in the way of normal life and the art projects never get done.

what do people hoard most?

- Clothes (often unworn with labels left on)
- Newspapers and magazines
- Containers
- Junk mail
- Books
- Craft items

are YOU A hoarder?

This questionnaire will help you work out, ahead of your challenge, if you are hoarding too many possessions or unwanted items in your home.
Score 2 points for a "Yes," 1 for a "Sometimes," and zero for a "No."

	Yes	Sometimes	No
1 Can you park your car in your garage, or is it too full of stuff?			
2 Are your bookshelves filled with books that you never read?			
3 Do you have piles of unread magazines and newspapers everywhere?			
4 Do you store unused or broken items under your bed?			
5 Are piles of junk mail left by your front door?			
6 Is your closet bulging with clothes that you don't wear?			
7 Is your purse, bag, or workbag full of old pens, receipts, candy wrappers, and other worthless trivia?			
8 Can you hardly get in your attic because you have so much stuff stored up there?			
9 Have you kept all your old school certificates or sports awards?			
10 Is your sock or pantyhose drawer so full you can hardly get it open?			
11 Do you have lots of framed photographs or art prints that have never been displayed stacked in a closet?			
12 Do you still keep shoes or boots even if you don't like them any more, they are badly worn, or have broken heels?			
13 Are you storing sports or fitness equipment that has never been used?			
14 Are you keeping photographs (prints or digital versions) of people who are no longer friends?			
15 Are unfinished craft projects scattered around your home?			
16 Is your home office full of paperwork that you have never got around to filing?			
17 Do you have old phones or broken electronic equipment stored in your home?			
18 Is your computer full of undeleted emails from months ago?			
19 Do you dislike some of the accessories or pictures in your home but never quite get around to disposing of them?			
20 Do you have any presents from friends or family, stored in the attic or a cabinet, that have never seen the light of day?			
TOTAL			

the results

30–40 Your hoarding tendencies are getting out of control. Start to look at ways of curbing your spending habits. You can now also pinpoint some of the key areas you will need to tackle first when you start the overall challenge of reducing all the possessions in your home. Become more ruthless in getting rid of things and ask yourself: Do I need, want, or use this?

20–29 Although hoarding is not a major problem for you, it could start to get out of control, so set a date to start offloading your superfluous possessions.

10–19 Hoarding is not a big issue for you yet. But do start looking at what you are willing to give away.

Below 10 You are not by habit a hoarder, so you should have no problem in releasing some possessions.

how TO become MORE minimalist

This can be daunting at first, as you will peel away emotional layers, removing items you have hung on to for years, but you will find it spiritually rewarding, and you will reinvent yourself as well as your home.

When you are going through the process of reducing all your belongings, and working on your 100-items list, focus on keeping the special things that remind you of happy times, and ones that you truly like or love, and use regularly—really think if you need that waffle pan or bread-maker you use once a year! The problem with hoarding too many old things is that they will strongly link you to your past, and will stop new things or people coming into your life. Stripping back your possessions can affect you profoundly (don't underestimate it), and can make you realize what is truly important in your life.

You need to keep items around you that foster and represent your current self, not the person you were years ago—bear this in mind when you are making your choices. All your possessions have an "energy" and those that are neglected or not used give off a stagnancy that can depress you. But the positive energy that comes from wanted or cherished objects will inspire you, help with your growth, and support your current dreams or goals.

letting go

If your home is really cluttered, try to think why you have surrounded yourself with so many things. Has it made you feel more protected? Many people hang on to possessions they no longer need or want because they are symbolically wrapping themselves up in "cotton wool" so that they do not move on or progress in life.

They may be doing this subconsciously, and once the possessions start to go, and these layers of "cotton wool" are removed, they can initially feel bereft and more exposed. But once they accept that the belongings have gone for good, a wonderful feeling of liberation can creep in. They no longer have to force themselves into cluttered rooms or spend hours searching for something that is hidden under piles of other stuff. If you have been feeling like this, just focus on all the new things you will be able to do when you have a clearer, more streamlined home.

GETTING GOING

Taking on the 100-item challenge, and letting other household possessions go, is a big step and it has to be taken when you are in the right frame of mind. So mentally prepare yourself for letting go of goods that you have kept for years. Try to start this kind of project when you are in a positive frame of mind because you will find it hard to let go of anything. Shortly before starting your challenge, choose a quiet weekend to look through old photo albums, pick up and hold accessories, and browse through some of the books on your shelves. Maybe spend some time trying on your old clothes and have fun remembering the old you, when you were younger, and the occasions when you wore the outfits. Allowing yourself time to reminisce about your belongings will make it easier to release some of them. It can be joyful to spend time looking through your possessions, even if you are letting them go.

finding joy

Make sorting through old photos and memorabilia a pleasurable experience. Take the time to reminisce and appreciate what your most valuable belongings mean to you.

appraising your home

View your home as a visitor would—try to look at everything in it with a dispassionate eye. Is it cozy but very cluttered? Do your books and old CDs and DVDs dominate your living room because you own so many of them? Do the countless accessories on the windowsill mean that you can hardly see the cherished photos of your family and friends? Has your love of magazines resulted in piles of them scattered all around the living room and entry hall? Is your kitchen a welcoming place or are the counters so full of appliances and products that it just looks too busy? This is the "heart" of the home, where people love to gather and chat, and it should be warm and inviting.

Move into the bedrooms and note any boxes you have stored on top of the closets. Are your clothes bulging out of the closets or drawers? Look under the beds—you may be surprised what forgotten junk has been stored under them. Are the toys in your kids' bedrooms out of control and scattered all around the room? Think about when you last gave any away to thrift (charity) stores or hospitals. Is your bathroom a soothing, relaxing place, or does it irritate you with the number of beauty products it contains? And are these strewn all around the bath or shower? Is your home study a pleasant place to enter or is it so full of paperwork, stationery, and office equipment that you feel overwhelmed? What about the attic? Can you get into it easily or is it an assault course, full of items that have just been dumped there and not used for years?

As you tour your home, really look at all your bits and pieces and ask yourself: Do I really like or love them? Do they bring me joy? Do I need them? You may be surprised at your reaction. Some items you once adored just may not appeal to you anymore. Remember that we all change and develop over time, so if you are surrounded with possessions that are, say, five to ten years old, you can find a mismatch of energies. These items are holding you in a past that you need to leave behind.

finding joy

Surrounding yourself only with things that match you and your family's current lifestyle will make you feel positive. It will give an energy boost and bring you pleasure.

releasing old or unwanted possessions

Ask yourself the following questions and if you answer "Yes" to most of
them, you definitely have items in your home that you need to release.

- Are there any items you have not used in
the last year?

- Do you have several broken articles that have
not been repaired?

- Have you got any inherited furniture that
you dislike?

- Do you dislike any possessions??

- Do you have things in your home that you
don't remember buying?

- Is your attic full of unwanted presents?

- Is it difficult to get into your attic space
because it is so full?

- Have your children got more toys than they
ever play with?

- Do you have books on your shelves that have
never been read?

- Have you got drawers full of old phones,
watches, or other paraphernalia?

PART 2

the 100-item challenge

Can you imagine living with just 100 personal possessions? This is the ultimate challenge I am giving you to live a simpler, more minimalist, and more joyful life. Making your list of personal possessions will highlight your buying weaknesses, and reducing it to 100 will force you to rationalize what is important to you. Setting separate goals for releasing your belongings is the ideal way to work through the challenge, so that you do not become too overwhelmed by the process. You will also feel good, knowing that either you will benefit financially from selling your possessions, or that you are helping others by donating them to worthy causes.

why take ON THE 100-item challenge?

Taking on the 100-item challenge is a positive step that will start you on the way to a simpler lifestyle with less stress and more time to contemplate your dreams and goals for the future. Having a picture of the life in front of you in your head, owning fewer possessions, will give you that impetus to get started.

Going around your home and really looking at everything you have will make you realize where your buying weaknesses lie. You may be a shopaholic for clothes, and love buying shoes, bags and purses, or jewelry. Maybe your obsession is your hobby and you love buying extras for your camera since photography is so important to you. It may prove hard at first but once you start shedding some of these possessions, you will start to feel lighter and happier as you lose the responsibility for looking after them. You will also notice an improvement in the atmosphere of your home, because having too many possessions creates a stagnancy, a dull atmosphere, that makes you feel sluggish and lacking in motivation. Removing a lot of them will bring about a positive shift in energy.

EMOTIONAL BENEFITS

You will become much more aware of what is important to you. Removing a lot of possessions from your life is similar to going off trekking or traveling for several months at a time. By cutting down, you will focus on what clothes you love and feel are essential, as well as on other items you use regularly and feel you can't do without. It will also make you realize that your love of life doesn't come from having

what will I gain from doing the 100-item challenge?

1 You will help to declutter your home.

2 You will have the goal of sticking to 100 personal possessions, even if you buy new things.

3 It will help you live a simpler, less stressful life.

4 It will make you focus on what possessions you feel are essential, what you love, and what you don't need.

5 You can have some fun testing your minimalist capabilities.

6 You will no longer be defined by your possessions.

7 You will be less obsessed with consumerism and will feel an improvement in your spiritual and emotional wellbeing.

8 Buying new items for the sake of it will become a thing of the past.

9 Your home will seem so much larger with more space in which to move around.

10 With fewer items in your home, the atmosphere will completely change and feel brighter and more uplifting.

a lot of possessions but from the activities you do and the time you spend with your family and friends. If you love painting or drawing, you may discover how important your art materials are to you; or it may be your hiking gear if you go on walking weekends with your local rambling group. You will find far more happiness in having a day out with your family, playing a sport, or catching up with friends than going on a mammoth shopping trip.

You may well fall in love with your home all over again as you liberate it from clutter. Clearing out will give you more space, and it will have an effect on you too, clearing and energizing your mind. As you let go of possessions that you may have held on to for many years, you may feel inspired to start hosting dinner parties again, having a games evening, or perhaps be the venue for the next book club meeting.

As you progress through the challenge, you will find yourself developing a much more disciplined attitude to buying, and may even start to find that browsing around the stores is less enjoyable. The other gain from doing the challenge is that consumer items will have less appeal when you experience the joy of all your other activities. Remember, too, that this is a challenge for a set period of time and you may decide not to continue with it at the end. However, your buying attitude will have changed forever and you will find you are far more careful about what you buy for your home.

Remember, this is your challenge. I am giving guidelines about what to do, but by all means adapt them to your needs. You can stretch the rules, or break some, if it keeps you more focused.

MY OWN 100-ITEM CHALLENGE

As part of my role as a feng shui consultant, I've spent many years helping people to declutter their homes, so I am used to the ethos of letting go of things you no longer need or want, and not overloading with possessions. However, when I decided to write this book and took on the challenge of trying to prune my own personal possessions down to 100, I must admit I was a bit worried. I live in Shoreham-by-Sea, on England's south coast, and the proximity of the stores in Brighton means I can easily go shopping for clothes, and since I moved here, my collection of clothes has grown considerably. This is the area I was concerned about—I love my clothes but am I really wearing all of them? And do they all reflect my current image? I do clear out quite regularly but I have fallen prey, like many people, to all the special offers. My journey, including all my ups and downs, to get down to 100 personal possessions is related in my journal, which I share with you throughout the book.

finding joy

Release the old item graciously.
If you find you need something similar
in the future, buying a new version
will bring joy and positivity.

my journal

I can't believe that I am about to start my 100-item challenge. Clothes are going to be the hardest group to pare down, because I seem to have acquired so many more since I left London to live by the sea. I don't live far from the shops in the trendy Lanes area of Brighton. Why do there have to be so many boutiques that just seem to call me in, knowing that I just love new boots, shoes, and bags? It's going to be a real test for me to be ruthless and let go of the ones I'm not using. I don't mind letting go of belongings, because decluttering is a regular part of my work, but it's so easy to clear out and then let stuff accumulate again. I will just have to keep saying to myself the mantra I say over and over to clients: Do I need it or want it?

Once I start, I find letting go is quite easy, but I still hesitate over the odd evening dress at the back of the closet. I don't wear them often now, but there might just be that special occasion… I will try them on and if I still look great in them, I will keep one or two.

Hobbies are not really my thing but I was a good tennis player in my day and I am keen to keep my tennis racket for the odd game, even though I don't play that much now. so I have quite a collection of workout gear that needs to be refined—do I really need that many T-shirts? I am feeling quite excited now but also a bit apprehensive about what's ahead. I know I will learn a lot from putting myself through this challenge.

WHERE DID THE 100-ITEM CHALLENGE START?

The concept of living with 100 personal possessions was the idea of online entrepreneur Dave Bruno, who looked around his San Diego home one day in 2007 and decided that all his family's belongings were weighing him down. So began his quest to reduce all his personal possessions to 100 items in a year. He reached his goal within that schedule, but continued his slow and steady purge of his items afterward.

The idea of living with fewer things is not new. Mahatma Gandhi (1869–1948), the non-violent leader of the Indian nationalist movement, adopted a very simple lifestyle, dressing in the clothes of an Indian villager. His own brief list of personal belongings included sandals, a plate, a bowl, his spectacles, and a pocket watch. In Britain, Guardian columnist Leo Hickman decided to work with the idea that a person needs just 10 belongings (excluding essential clothing and household goods). His list included a Swiss army knife and a treasured painting by one of his children.

When I conceived the idea for this book, I wanted to bring in the idea of a 100-item challenge in a workbook style, so I could provide some guidance on decluttering. Clearing out all unnecessary household goods is essential for changing a life of over-consumerism, but focusing on reducing your own belongings is a much harder test and a more personal experience.

Letting go of your own possessions is never easy, but once you start cutting that tie with them it can be liberating. When you release surplus items, everything that you keep will have special meaning and purpose. You are going to hit some rough patches during the challenge, so if you are finding it tough, give yourself a day or two off and come back mentally revitalized and emotionally refreshed.

making your 100-item list

I have been inspired to take on the 100-item challenge through my work as a decluttering consultant. Having seen many clients over the years who have filled their homes with too many possessions, I was curious to test myself and see how minimalist I could be with my personal belongings.

By "items," or personal possessions, I mean all the items that you own and use, for example, your computer and your clothes. All household goods that are used by your family and friends, such as furniture, electrical items in shared areas, and china, are excluded from the challenge. However, some of these still need to be cleared out, and advice on decluttering every room is covered in Part 3.

Taking on the challenge is a strict discipline but it is also fun and will highlight how much money you can waste buying what are basically unwanted or frivolous goods. The challenge is also about acquiring a more spacious, clutter-free home, and having more spare time and money to pursue the activities you love.

HOW TO ORGANIZE YOUR LIST

Remember, this is a challenge that is good for the soul, so you can set your own rules, provided that you keep to them for your specified time. You may decide to try it for a year or 18 months and then review it. It is also your choice how to count items. It is sensible to group some. You may decide that your collection of purses (handbags) is so huge that it's best to group them as one, but nevertheless, always aim to reduce the number that you have. It is also a good idea to group all underwear, and socks and pantyhose as one item, or you will never achieve your 100 items! I have decided to group my shoes as one item but will cut back on my collection. Achieving your 100 items will make you feel very self-disciplined.

When making your list, leave some room for gifts that may come your way. You can still buy clothes or new items, as long as they don't put your list over 100, and you can replace anything that's worn-out or broken. You can also allow yourself one indulgence that is excluded from the challenge. Mine is going to be my jewelry collection. I just love bright crystal pieces to match my outfits.

So whether you are single, one of a couple, or part of a family, before you get going set some ground rules.

what is excluded

- All general or shared household items. This means furniture, such as sofas, chairs, and beds, and electrical items, such as televisions, fridge/freezers, stoves, microwaves, and kettles
- All china and glasses
- All basic food items
- Tool kits and home repair (DIY) items
- Household cleaning materials
- Soft furnishings and bedlinen
- Stationery and home-office furniture and supplies
- Books
- DVDs and CDs
- Cars
- Shampoos, conditioners, and other shared bathroom products

what is included

- Clothes: general items, nightwear, shoes, sandals, boots, gloves, coats, jackets, scarves, belts, ties, hats, and wraps
- Jewelry
- Cosmetics, including nail scissors, nail varnishes, and tweezers
- Toothbrushes, razors, aftershaves, perfumes, and moisturizers
- Personal hair dryer, hair straighteners, and curlers
- Personal computer, laptop, and printer
- Phone, camera, headphones, electronic items, including tablets, e-readers, games consoles
- Watches, clocks, penknives, sunglasses, and spectacles
- Hobby items, such as personal musical instruments, photography equipment, train sets, sketch pads and paints, and craft and knitting kits
- Bicycle or motorbike and helmet
- Suitcases, purses, backpacks, bags, workbags, and wallets
- Notepads, journals, pens, and pencils
- Sports gear, such as tennis rackets, golf clubs, surfboards, football gear, running equipment, and skateboards

These lists are just a guide so if you have something personal that is not here and you feel should be included, add it.

what POSSESSIONS CAN'T you live WITHOUT?

Fill in this questionnaire to find out what are your essential items.
Score 2 points for a "Yes," 1 for a "Sometimes," and zero for a "No."

	Yes	Sometimes	No
1 Do your headphones/earbuds have to go everywhere with you?			
2 Are you completely lost without your laptop?			
3 Do you have special boots that you always choose to wear?			
4 If you lost your cherished leather jacket, would you be mortified?			
5 Do you freak out if you realize that you have left your e-reader at home?			
6 If your beloved black trousers are in the wash, are you at a loss for what to wear?			
7 Do you start to panic if you can't find your phone?			
8 Are you constantly checking all your meetings and arrangements in your diary?			
9 Does your makeup bag have to go everywhere with you so that you can easily touch up your lip gloss or mascara?			
10 Do you take your backpack with you at all times, and feel lost without it?			
11 Do you wear the same piece or pieces of jewelry every day?			
12 Is it upsetting to find you have no time to change your purse (bag) to match your outfit?			
13 Do you always carry a big wallet, even though you hardly ever carry cash?			
14 Do your friends recognize you from a distance, because you always wear the same jacket when you are out?			
15 In the summer, are you lost if you leave your designer sunglasses behind?			
16 Is your gym bag always packed and ready for your next workout session?			
17 Do you regularly rotate three or four shirts or T-shirts to wear?			
18 Are you at a loss if you can't find your notebook and pen to make notes to yourself?			
19 Do you keep your golf clubs, tennis racket, or squash racket by the door, ready for the next game?			
20 Do you feel almost undressed if you don't wear your preferred hat when you go out?			
TOTAL			

the results

30–40 You have a lot of possessions that are an essential part of your life. Since all of these count toward your list of 100 items, you may need to toughen up so that you are ready to release other less important belongings. Focus on what you really want and need in your life.

20–29 Although your list of loved belongings is not enormous, the 100-item challenge will still be tough, so start to get into the mindset of letting go of all your unnecessary possessions.

10–19 Attachment to personal possessions is not a huge problem for you, but start reviewing which ones you really want to keep.

Below 10 You do not seem to have too much attachment to your belongings, and should find the challenge quite easy to undertake.

taking AN inventory OF YOUR personal possessions

Before you can start the challenge, you need to take an inventory of all the things you own that you alone use, and start noting down your feelings about releasing them. Remember that general household goods are excluded from this list (see page 33). Allow some time, because it can take a while to log everything. You may be horrified at how much you have accumulated or pleasantly surprised that it is not as much as you thought.

Before you make your list, decide what possessions you are going to write down individually, and what you are going to group together as one item, to make your task easier. For example, are you going to list your shoes and boots pair by pair or as one or two groups? Are you going to put your purses (handbags) down separately or as a group? You may decide to put belts down as one or two group items. It's your decision. I think it's sensible to make more group items if it means that you will keep to the challenge.

Write your list on a large lined pad and have a selection of colored pens, including black, so you can color-code your decisions about what to keep and what to move on. When you have finished, pin the pad somewhere you will see it every day, such as on the fridge door.

WHERE TO BEGIN?

I suggest you start in your bedroom, if that is where you keep your clothes, because they will make up around 70 percent of your challenge items. List them all, including footwear, using a black pen—this is all your summer and winter clothes, and your fat and thin clothes, if you have them! If any are stored in boxes on top of the closet or under the bed, add them in as well. Don't forget to include any clothes that you wear infrequently, such as ski wear or party dresses, which may be stored away in the attic. All your coats, jackets, scarves, and hats, which may be hanging downstairs or by the front door, should be included, too.

If you are struggling to make decisions about what to keep and what to lose, it may be an idea to invite a friend for the afternoon to help you decide. A friend who is not emotionally attached to your clothes will be able to say more honestly what

flatters you and what doesn't suit you or, possibly, fit you anymore. Remember, this is your inventory so you can have several "don't knows" if you need more time to let go of some old favorites.

While in this room, add to your list any electrical items, such as hair dryers, hair straighteners, shavers, or alarm clocks that are personal to you. Don't forget to make it clear what are your essentials that you can't do without. Add your cosmetics, perfumes, purses (handbags), bags, and jewelry to the list.

ALL YOUR OTHER BELONGINGS

Move on from your bedroom and note down all your personal electronic items, such as laptops, mobile printers (exclude big home-office equipment, like a photocopier), phones, e-readers, and tablets. If you have several old models, note these down and mark them as "can go"—you can probably sell them or pass them on to other people.

Look at any hobby items you may have. Do you have lots of craft equipment and tools, say for making rugs or jewelry? They all need to be recorded. If you are a sports lover, all your equipment must be listed—tennis rackets and balls, hockey sticks, weight-training kit, skateboards, and any other gear must be added.

Finally, add the small miscellaneous possessions—your wallet, penknife, sunglasses, notepad or journal and pen, watches, even your toothbrush. If you have a bicycle or motorbike, add it in.

If you are feeling a bit shell-shocked by the length of your list, don't forget you can still exclude one indulgence item or group from your challenge. Also, remember the aim of the challenge is to get down to 100 items, but if you get stuck at 150, store the ones you just can't relinquish in the attic or a closet until the end of the challenge. If you have missed them, you may well get them out again, but if not, move them on.

Check through your list and make sure you haven't left anything out before filling in the current personal possessions list on pages 40–43, followed by your proposed list of 100 items on pages 44–45. You are now well on the way to achieving your new minimalist lifestyle.

While you are taking your inventory of all your clothes, gadgets, and other belongings, write next to each item in red if it is a "must have," in blue for a "don't know," and in green for "can go." You may find that a lot of the "can gos" appear next to clothes. Other items, such as your laptop, are probably essential to you. When you start the Goals section (see pages 46–65), review the list and make your final decisions to get down to your 100 items.

your current list of personal items

FIRST INVENTORY Fill in your inventory list here, and total up what you have. Don't forget to exclude all household goods and to group underwear, and pantyhose and socks. If you have too many possessions to fit on these two spreads, continue on another piece of paper.

Gadgets & miscellaneous

_____

_____

_____

_____

_____

_____

_____

_____

_____

_____

_____

_____

_____

_____

_____

_____

_____

_____

_____

_____

_____

_____

Winter clothes

_____

_____

_____

_____

_____

_____

_____

_____

_____

_____

_____

_____

_____

_____

_____

_____

_____

_____

_____

_____

_____

Summer clothes

your current list of personal items continued

Gadgets & miscellaneous

Winter clothes

Summer clothes

_____ _____
_____ _____
_____ _____
_____ _____
_____ _____
_____ _____
_____ _____
_____ _____
_____ _____
_____ _____
_____ _____
_____ _____
_____ _____
_____ _____
_____ _____
_____ _____
_____ _____
_____ _____
_____ _____

Total

Gadgets & miscellaneous.....................................

Winter clothes..

Summer clothes..

Total items..

your 100-item list

Remember you can allow yourself up to a year, or longer, to achieve this number. The main reason for compiling this list is to get into the mindset to let go of things. Group items together if you are finding it just too hard. It is your challenge and you can make your own rules.

Gadgets & miscellaneous

Winter clothes

Summer clothes

Total

goal setting

Now you have planned your 100-item list, how are you going to achieve it? Setting goals within a time scale is the best way. If you are not good at letting things go, you may find this quite difficult to do but, I promise you, you will feel better at the end of it. Refining your possessions down to those that you really love and want can focus you both mentally and emotionally. And what are all those things that you never use doing? Basically, they are just gathering dust and using up space in your home. Too often people hang on to things they do not use or want through inertia or lethargy—they have just got used to those things being there. By moving them on, you will create an atmosphere that is much more positive and vibrant, which everyone in your family will notice and appreciate. Also, exciting new things can come into your life after a clear-out, when the energy in your home is boosted.

MAKING YOUR PLAN

To keep on track, make sure the goals and time limits you set yourself are achievable. A year is a good target to set. If you feel you can do it in less time, that's fine, but if you are really overloaded with stuff, you may feel 18 months is more realistic. I have set myself a year to reach my target of 100 items. I think I will get there more quickly than that but may get stuck on losing the last 50 items, which I still love and want to keep. Work out your goals chart (see the sample chart opposite), print it out with the timings involved, and display it in a prominent place where you will see it every day. As you reach each goal, cross through it with a colored pen and feel that sense of achievement. If you are feeling a bit daunted, think of it as a fun game where you are testing yourself to see how few things you can live with.

If you are working to a year's schedule, make sure you plan how many months to allow for reducing your collection of clothes, for example. In my sample plan, I suggest that Goal 1 should be working on your clothes; Goal 2 can be your shoes, boots, bags, wallets, and suitcases; Goal 3 your jewelry, cosmetics, perfumes, aftershaves, and miscellaneous possessions; and Goal 4 your electronic items. Goal 5 can be your sports goods, and Goal 6 your hobby materials. If you have other things that do not fit into these categories, just add them to your chart. As your clothes will make up about 70 percent of your final list of 100, it is a good idea to allow more time to clear out your closet. Adopt the mantra "love it, use it, or lose it" for everything you own to help you make your decisions.

USING YOUR CHART

You will find it helpful to display your chart on your fridge door, on the closet in your bedroom, or in any other prominent position where you can't ignore it. Decide your start month and how many months you are giving yourself to work on the first goal, then fill in the next goal, and so on. If you find you are going to need more time to complete each goal, just change the dates on your chart.

sample goal-setting chart

In this example I have allowed 4½ months to pare down clothes and 1½ months each for the other more minor goals.

	Start date	Completion date
1st goal: All clothes	end July	mid-December
2nd goal: Shoes, boots, wallets, purses, bags, suitcases	mid-December	end January
3rd goal: Jewelry, cosmetics, miscellaneous possessions	end January	mid-March
4th goal: Electronic items	mid-March	end April
5th goal: Sports equipment	end April	mid-June
6th goal: Hobby materials	mid-June	end July

goal 1: clothes
TIME TO COMPLETE: 4½ MONTHS

This is your first goal and the biggest part of your 100-item challenge because it deals with all your clothes, which will make up a major part of your list. I have allocated a fair bit of time to achieving this goal, but once you start removing clothes from where you store them, you may find you can complete the task more quickly. You may have decided to leave filling in your proposed list of 100 items (see pages 44–45) until you have worked through these clearing-out goals.

Getting rid of clothes you have had for a while can be quite a difficult process. They remind us of the happy times when we wore them. As you sort through them you may remember an event such as your sister's wedding or a party where you had a great time. Clothes can often seem like friends because they are so much a part of us. They represent our personal style, and the image we are projecting to the world. However, letting go of clothes you no longer need or want can be liberating, and can stop you from being too tied to the past or to the person you were a few years ago. It is also worthwhile noting that most of us regularly wear just 20 percent of our clothes; the rest just hang in the closet, filling up space. If you weaken at any time, don't forget that the focus of this challenge is to discover the joy of living with fewer things.

LETTING GO

To start the process of living with fewer clothes and having a "capsule" wardrobe of your favorite items, get together some heavy-duty trash bags. Label the first bag "Thrift (charity) store and friends" (you may need several of these). Label the second bag "Clothes to sell." If you have some really old clothes, you may want to add a third junk bag labeled "Clothes to throw out." Inviting friends to a clothes-exchange party can be a fun idea, so label another bag "Clothes to exchange."

Now look at the inventory you made earlier (see pages 40–43) and, following the checklist order opposite, start working through your clothes. Allocate a few hours at a time and stop when you feel you can't do any more. Start with the "can go" clothes on your inventory and put them in the appropriate trash bags. Next, start work on your "don't know" list of clothes. You may have tried on some of these but still can't make a decision about letting them go. Give yourself a bit of time—it's not an easy process. You may have to come back to some of these on another day if you can't make up your mind. Finally, look at your "must have" list of clothes. You may find when you total up all of these that you still have too many for your 100 list and will have to refine them even more.

Once you have let go of your clothes and they are bagged up, make sure you move them on quickly, to the thrift (charity) or secondhand store, for example, or the temptation will be to start rooting through the bags again and putting some things back in the closet. Your subconscious will try to convince you that you can't possibly do without that particular dress or jacket!

CHECKLIST

To keep you on track, it can help to go through your clothes in a set order, otherwise you may become overwhelmed by the task ahead. If you don't have any of the clothes in one of the sections listed, just skip to the next one. If you have something to add, just write it on a piece of paper. Go through both your winter and summer clothes at the same time.

Women

1 Skirts
2 Dresses
3 Shirts
4 Pants (trousers)
5 Jeans
6 Long-sleeved T-shirts
7 Sweaters
8 Short-sleeved shirts
9 Short-sleeved T-shirts
10 Vest T-shirts
11 Strappy T-shirts
12 Shorts
13 Cropped pants
14 Cardigans/shrugs
15 Fleeces
16 Evening tops
17 Pantyhose/socks
18 Bras
19 Panties
20 Pjs
21 Nightdresses
22 Bathrobes
23 Gym shorts/leggings
24 Gym T-shirts
25 Bikinis and swimsuits
26 Coats
27 Jackets
28 Rain jackets
29 Scarves and wraps
30 Hats
31 Gloves
32 Belts
33 Miscellaneous

Men

1 Suits
2 Shirts
3 Ties
4 Pants (trousers)
5 Jeans
6 Long-sleeved T-shirts
7 Sweaters/sweater vests
8 Short-sleeved shirts
9 Short-sleeved T-shirts
10 Vest T-shirts
11 Shorts
12 Cropped pants
13 Cardigans
14 Fleeces
15 Socks
16 Underwear
17 Pjs
18 Bathrobes
19 Gym shorts/pants
20 Gym T-shirts
21 Swimsuits
22 Coats
23 Jackets
24 Rain jackets
25 Scarves
26 Hats
27 Gloves
28 Belts
29 Miscellaneous

By keeping only the clothes that you like and look good wearing, you will boost your self-esteem and confidence. And giving clothes away to a worthy cause will make you feel good about yourself.

TOO MANY CLOTHES?

Now that you are looking at all your clothes and deciding what to keep and what to let go, it is interesting to look at the reasons why we hang on to clothes we no longer wear. Many people have a vast collection of clothes of all types and colors, so how is it that, according to statistics, most of us wear just 20 percent of all the clothes we own? Do we buy clothes for the sake of it and then forget about them? Is it laziness? I know that when the weather is cold in the winter, I can easily just rotate between two pairs of jeans and two or three sweaters if I'm feeling lazy. Do we just wear the clothes that are nearest in the closet and forget about the rest? Do we buy too many clothes and forget what we have? Or is it that some don't fit or we just don't like them any more? Perhaps some people feel more secure with more clothes to choose from, but whatever the reason or reasons may be, isn't it a waste of money to have so many clothes that are not worn?

I decided to conduct an experiment with three friends by asking them to keep a winter clothes diary over a working week to see if they wore a mixture of clothes and footwear, or chose the same ones regularly, and if the reason for that was because it required less effort. Have a look at the results on the pages that follow.

ANNA

Anna works in a London office as an accountant.

MONDAY: Blue dress, black knitted jacket, black ankle boots.

TUESDAY: Printed skirt, black T-shirt, black ankle boots.

WEDNESDAY: Black shift dress, black knitted jacket, black ankle boots.

THURSDAY: Black jeggings, black T-shirt (different one), black knitted jacket.

FRIDAY: Blue jeans, green top, full-length black boots.

Anna wore several black pieces of clothing, and has chosen few colorful items for her weekly wardrobe. She also wore the same pair of ankle boots for four days in the week.

energy booster

Anna needs to wear more of the boots and shoes in her wardrobe or move them on. Black is smart but wearing her colorful tops or skirts will boost her energy.

SARAH

Sarah has a job in marketing and generally works in an office during the week.

MONDAY: Brown polo neck sweater, brown pants, bright orange cardigan, brown suede boots.

TUESDAY: Gray polo neck sweater, gray pants, red wrap-style cardigan, gray flat shoes in patent leather.

WEDNESDAY: Brown polo neck sweater, brown pants, bright orange cardigan, brown suede boots.

THURSDAY: Black fleck pant suit, green sweater, black high boots.

FRIDAY: Gray polo neck sweater, gray pants, lilac cardigan, gray flat shoes in patent leather.

Sarah repeats clothes in her week's selection. She also admits she chooses clothes that are easy to find on dark winter mornings.

more versatility

Sarah could be more versatile with her choices, and wear more of her other tops and coordinates. Choosing her clothes the night before will solve finding things on dark mornings.

LUCY

Lucy works from home as a holistic healer.

MONDAY: Black jeans, animal-print top, long black cardigan, black boots.

TUESDAY: Black leggings, green T-shirt, animal-print tie cardigan, black boots.

WEDNESDAY: Black jeans, animal-print T-shirt, long black cardigan, black boots.

THURSDAY: Black jeans, stripy T-shirt, long black cardigan, black boots.

FRIDAY: Black leggings, knitted animal-print dress, black boots.

Lucy regularly chooses black clothes as an easy option. There is also a big emphasis on animal prints, despite owning many other different styles. She also chose to wear the same pair of black boots all week.

color burst

Lucy needs to wear more of the other boots and shoes in her wardrobe for variety. Wearing more colorful tops and cardigans would be a good idea.

WARDROBE CHALLENGES

Appraising your wardrobe before embarking on the 100-item challenge can take a while. You may find your closet is full of clothes that you do not wear, some hidden, still with their labels on, plus other items that are too tight and no longer fit.

The idea of the challenge is to pare down your wardrobe to only the clothes that you love and want, clothes you feel good in and wear regularly. Once you have sorted your clothes, you can color-code them as shirts, skirts, pants etc, so that they can be easily picked out and matched together, particularly on those dark winter mornings. All the unwanted clothes can be passed on to friends or thrift (charity) stores, or sold through secondhand stores or online.

If you are not a tidy individual, there may be piles of clothes at the bottom of the closet to sort through. Old and damaged clothes may have been discarded and forgotten about. Discard that gray underwear and the single socks that have lost their matching partner!

finding joy

The purpose of the challenge is to keep only the clothes that you wear often and love, the clothes that are stylish and which make you feel good about yourself.

goal 2: shoes, boots, bags, wallets, and suitcases
TIME TO COMPLETE: 1½ MONTHS

The second goal of your 100-item challenge is to deal with all your shoes, boots, purses (handbags), bags, wallets, and suitcases. I find this goal quite hard, because I love my collection of bags. I will have to be really tough with myself to let go of the ones I'm just not using anymore. I also seem to have acquired a suitcase for every occasion—how many do you need? I will just have to be realistic and keep only the ones I use. Less time is needed to achieve this goal because there are fewer possessions to deal with.

Having the right shoes and purse (handbag) can make an outfit special. But if you have bought freely for years, your closets are probably full of shoes, boots, and bags that you haven't worn or carried for a while. You may feel you still love a lot of these possessions but if you are not using or wearing them, they are just cluttering up your bedroom. They may also relate to the "old" you, who possibly liked bolder styles than you do today. Throwing out battered shoes, purses (handbags), and bags, and taking those that are in good condition to thrift (charity) or secondhand stores will make you feel good and create a workable collection that relates to your current style and energy. There is less emotion attached to wallets, suitcases, or workbags, but you still have to make your final selection.

checklist

Go through all your shoes, boots, purses (handbags), bags, wallets, and suitcases in this order, and avoid flitting between closets and drawers.

1 Shoes (all formal and casual styles, high heels, and flats)
2 Boots
3 Sandals, flip-flops, swimming shoes
4 Sneakers, running shoes, walking and hiking boots
5 Purses (handbags)
6 Small evening bags
7 Wallets
8 Workbags
9 Backpacks
10 Suitcases or travel bags
11 Miscellaneous accessories, such as sunglasses and spectacles

LETTING GO

As with your clothes, use heavy-duty trash bags and label them appropriately (see page 48). Work swiftly through your inventory (see pages 40–43), looking at your "can go" list, then your "don't knows," and finally your "must have" items. Use the checklist to keep you focused but change the heading to "Goal 2." You may need a third bag labeled "Miscellaneous—to throw out."

finding joy

Having less will make you fully appreciate the belongings you have kept. You will derive great pleasure from sorting and co-ordinating the bags and shoes you have, knowing that you've held on to those that you like the best.

goal 3: jewelry, cosmetics, and miscellaneous items
TIME TO COMPLETE: 1½ MONTHS

Your third goal is sorting out jewelry, cosmetics, and other miscellaneous bits and pieces. I love my jewelry so have made it my indulgence, but I am still going to sort through every piece and make sure I still love and wear it, or I will pass it on. Again, this goal has a shorter completion time because there are fewer items you need to go through.

A stunning necklace, bracelet, or ring makes you feel special, but today it is all too easy to buy cheap costume jewelry on a whim, and then rarely wear it. So if your jewelry box and hanging trees are overflowing, you may need some time to look through everything and decide what to keep. If you have some gold pieces that you never wear, selling them can be a good option (see page 68) since gold usually fetches a high price. You may come across items you have been given as presents that stimulate happy memories, or make you feel emotional, but hard as it is, try to put emotion aside. As with everything else, focus on what you love wearing, and which pieces make you feel good. Don't forget to include all your watches.

With cosmetics, the aim is to end up with just one makeup bag for all the eye shadows, eye pencils, liquid liners, blushers, brushes, mascaras, nail varnishes, creams, and lotions that you use regularly. Get rid of all those clogged-up old cosmetics, as well as any that are stored elsewhere. Don't forget to sort through your moisturizers and perfumes or aftershaves.

checklist

Keep focused by working through your jewelry and cosmetics in this order.

Jewelry

1 Necklaces/pendants
2 Bracelets/anklets
3 Earrings
4 Watches
5 Miscellaneous jewelry

Cosmetics

6 Eye shadows/creams
7 Blushers and brushes
8 Touch-up creams/foundations/powders
9 Mascaras
10 Eye pencils/liners
11 Lipsticks/lipgloss
12 Moisturizers/serums
13 Nail varnishes
14 Miscellaneous items plus nail scissors, tweezers, and eyelash curlers
15 Fragrances

REFINING YOUR COLLECTION

With this goal I suggest using a couple of small boxes (something like a shoe box) for your jewelry. Label one "Thrift (charity) store and friends" and label the other "Jewelry to sell." Have a junk bag labeled "Cosmetics, lotions, and fragrances to throw out."

Work through your inventory (see pages 40–43), going through your "can go" list, "don't knows," and your "must have" items, although in this section you may have left it until now to make final choices.

finding joy

Once you have reduced your jewelry collection down to the few items you truly love and treasure, consider having them cleaned or cleaning them yourself to bring some true sparkle and joy into your life.

goal 4: electrical and electronic equipment
TIME TO COMPLETE: 1½ MONTHS

Your fourth goal may be a problem if you love gadgets. I have not acquired too many of them but the challenge has spurred me on to sell my old phone and to give my old computer to a charity that will re-use it and clear your hard drive at the same time. Again, there is a shorter time to reach this goal because of fewer gadgets to review.

Electronic gadgets are the obsession of the 21st century. When a new version of a gadget is announced, people often line up overnight to make sure they are among the first to own it. So what has fueled this demand for new gadgets? Is it material consumerism gone mad? Or is it just a fascination for new technology? There is no doubt that modern electronic appliances ease the running of our daily lives but there is also the slight worry that we can never switch off, because we are always contactable. If you are looking at the electrical and electronic items you own and wondering how to reduce them for this challenge, try to think what you use or play with daily, and what is indispensable. Try to stay focused on how you are streamlining and simplifying your life when doing this challenge.

RELEASING GADGETS

As this goal involves appliances, find some boxes and label them "Thrift (charity) stores and friends" (not all stores accept electrical and electronic devices), "Gadgets to sell," and "Gadgets to throw out."

Go through your inventory (see pages 40–43), starting with your "can go" list followed by your "don't knows." You may struggle here, feeling unsure whether to release once-loved appliances—give yourself time to let them go. When you are ready, move on to your "must have" devices.

checklist

Use this list to go through all your current devices and electrical appliances in order.

1 Computers/laptops
2 Printers
3 External hard drives
4 Phones
5 Headphones
6 Speakers
7 E-readers
8 Tablets
9 Games consoles
10 Electric razor
11 Hair dryers
12 Hair straighteners and curling tongs
13 Miscellaneous gadgets including clocks

finding joy

While you're doing an inventory of your gadgets, discover the joy of having a digital detox and allowing yourself some screen-free time.

goal 5: sports and exercise equipment

TIME TO COMPLETE: 1½ MONTHS

Your fifth goal is to check your sports equipment. My bicycle is a "must have"—one of the pleasures of living by the sea is cycling along the coast during the summer months. Six weeks is the time allowed for this goal, which should be ample to rationalize all your sports paraphernalia.

For sports lovers, this is decision time. You may be keeping some equipment that you just don't use any more. Did you take up a sport, such as badminton, but gave it up after the initial enthusiasm wore off, and left the racket languishing in your attic? Or maybe you tried canoeing or sailing but discovered that a life on the water wasn't for you? All this wasted equipment can be sold on auction websites, such as ebay. Alternatively, you can donate it to a youth club or sports club, who will appreciate the gift of hardly used equipment. By giving these things away, you will not only end up with your favorite items, creating good energy in your home, but you will also feel good about helping others.

LIBERATING SPORTS EQUIPMENT

Use some heavy-duty trash bags. Label one "Youth club, sports club, or friends," and label another "Sports goods to sell." For any old unused equipment, label a third bag "Sports goods to throw out."

Tackle the sports section of your inventory (see pages 40–43), starting with your "can go" list, and then move on to the "don't knows"—just release unused sports items. Lastly, sort out all your favorites in the "must have" selection.

finding joy

Perhaps during this part of the challenge you can rediscover the love of a sport you haven't played for some time, or set yourself the challenge of finding a new, fun activity to try.

checklist

Sort through your sports and exercise equipment as listed, to keep you on track with your clear-out.

1 Tennis rackets and balls
2 Badminton rackets and shuttlecocks
3 Squash rackets and balls
4 Golf clubs and golf balls
5 Skateboard
6 Surfboard
7 Running equipment
8 Weight-training belts and dumbbells

9 Hockey stick
10 Soccer and equipment
11 Swimming equipment
12 Bicycle
13 Cycling gear
14 Motorbike
15 Motorbike equipment
16 Aerobics/workout gear

17 Yoga mat and equipment
18 Pilates kit
19 Hiking or walking gear
20 Sailing kit
21 Camping equipment
22 Canoeing gear
23 Miscellaneous sports equipment, including penknives

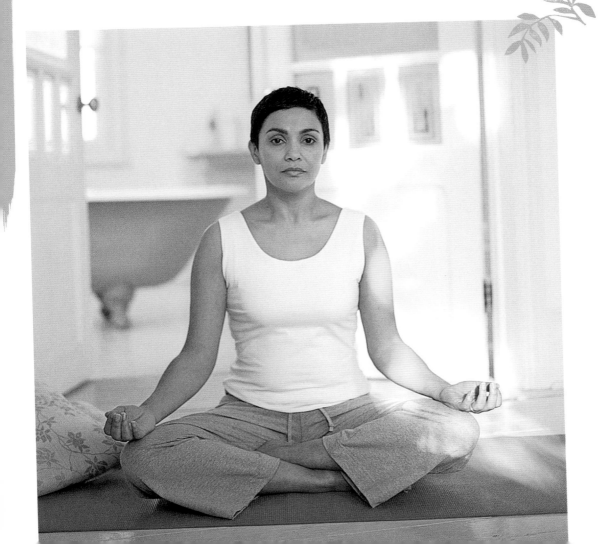

goal 6: hobby materials

TIME TO COMPLETE: 1½ MONTHS

The final goal of your 100-item challenge is to review your hobby materials. All those odd bits and pieces such as notepads and journals are included with this goal. I am not a great hobby person but I do really love drawing and painting, so these art materials are among my "must haves." Sketching outside is one of my enjoyments.

Hobbies can be addictive—once you take up one, you just want to start more. But if you get bored quickly, it will mean that you have a lot of half-finished projects around. You may have tried a ceramics course, making jewelry, or maybe something like stained-glass work. Photography is an amazing hobby but you can acquire a lot of equipment that you may not get around to using. Perhaps you thought you were going to develop your own black-and-white prints and bought all the materials but then never had the time? All this kit is taking up space in your home. If you are an amateur musician, you probably have several instruments that you have bought over the years, but do you still play them all? When did you last play that guitar or keyboard? Online auction sites and secondhand stores are ideal places to sell on unwanted expensive hobby items. Or you could donate some cameras or musical instruments to amateur clubs, which would really appreciate them. Helping people can be incredibly rewarding, and can make you appreciate how lucky you are and how much you have in your life.

RELINQUISHING HOBBY MATERIALS

Again, use some heavy-duty trash bags. Label one "Amateur clubs or friends," and another "Hobby equipment to sell." For any old craft or hobby items, label a third bag "Hobby materials to throw out."

Sort through your inventory (see pages 40–43), moving through your "can go" list, your "don't knows," and, finally, check through your "must have" pieces.

checklist

Work through all your hobby items in this order to speed up the process.

1 Art materials
2 Craft kits
3 Gardening kit
4 Ceramic materials
5 Photography equipment
6 Stamp collections
7 Glass-making kits
8 Jewelry-making kits
9 Knitting paraphernalia
10 Sewing kits
11 Language disks
12 Guitar
13 Keyboard/piano
14 Trumpet
15 Saxophone
16 Flute/recorder
17 Train sets
18 Miscellaneous musical instruments
19 Journals, notepads, and pens
20 Diaries
21 Miscellaneous hobby items

finding joy

Which hobby items were you excited to discover beneath the clutter? Can you dust them down and revive your interest?

my journal

My bedroom looks like a bombsite! Practically everything I own is scattered around as I look through everything. I have just read that the average British woman has 22 items of clothing that she never wears but refuses to throw out because of the guilt of wasting money! Thankfully, that is not my problem, but I have just discovered two black Tula bags in the top of my closet that I haven't used in over a year, so they are going to the secondhand store that has just opened at the end of my road—maybe I can earn some cash from them? Apparently, too many of us buy clothes for our slimmer, sexier persona, and they just end up sitting at the back of the closet. I am not guilty of that but I do love those offers on T-shirts…

Out, too, go my beige boots that seem to have worn down more on one foot than the other, making them so uncomfortable to wear now. My black biker boots can go as well—they just don't seem to be me any more. Oh good, a charity bag for breast cancer has just come through the door. I can fill it up with my reject scarves plus a waterproof jacket and some other bits. Still a long way to go, but it does feel good donating things I no longer need to a good cause.

selling OR donating YOUR belongings

If you keep tripping over piles of garbage bags full of your discarded belongings because you have kept them rather than moving them on as you have gone along, there are several ways you can sell or donate your belongings.

Clothes are ideal to sell to regular secondhand, or secondhand designer, stores or through an online auction site. Thrift (charity) stores are usually grateful for any good-quality clothes, if you want to donate them. Many jewelry stores buy secondhand items, particularly rings, so it is worth checking prices with a few before you sell. Several online gold stores buy gold jewelry, even if it is broken, paying you by the carat and the weight of the pieces. Secondhand stores will buy electrical or electronic goods, particularly laptops, photographic equipment, and phones. They are also interested in sports equipment and musical instruments. In the US there are online companies that buy sports equipment that is in good condition. Several online stores will buy your old phone—you just key in the model number and they will give you a price.

If these outlets don't work for you, consider taking a pitch at a car boot sale or have a garage or yard sale, but bear in mind you have to price things quite low to attract the customers. Advertising in local papers, which may be free for small items, can also prove successful, as well as on social media sites. Specialist clubs, sports clubs, youth clubs, and local schools will often welcome donations of equipment that is in good condition. Visit them to ask if they are interested in what you want to donate. Otherwise, there are websites that will recycle pieces for you.

Don't feel sad at the loss of some of the things you owned. Use the cash you have made from selling them to take a trip, do something you have always wanted to do, meet friends for a meal, or treat your family to the theater or to a movie. Remember, too, that by donating some of your possessions to clubs or thrift (charity) stores, they will go to other people who will use them and love them.

selling

CLOTHES

Many secondhand clothes stores, and secondhand designer label clothes stores, exist throughout Britain; a few are detailed here. Customers selling clothes or accessories are often paid after the item is sold. Shops normally take goods on a sale or return basis and pay commission of around 50 percent of the agreed price.

Cinderella's Dress Agency
www.cinderellasdressagency.co.uk
52a Shaw Road, Stockport
SK4 4AL.
0161 432 3496
Buys and sells high-street and designer wear.

Designs
www.designsnw3.uk
60 Rosslyn Hill, Belsize Park, London NW3 1ND.
020 7435 0100
Buys and sells secondhand designer clothes.

The Dresser
www.dresseronline.co.uk
10 Porchester Place, Connaught Village, London W2 2BS.
020 7724 7212
Higher-end designer clothes agency, specializing in the buying and selling of contemporary and couture secondhand designer women's and menswear. They take items on a sale or return basis, and charge a 50 percent commission.

MUSICAL INSTRUMENTS

www.whybuynew.co.uk
This online store buys secondhand musical instruments. Call or email detailing what you have to sell. Agree on the price quoted, pack your item carefully, and arrange safe transport, or they will pick up by courier for a fee. Once the instrument is received and inspected, which takes between 24 and 48 hours, they will arrange payment via BACS transfer. They will also buy computers, laptops, and cell phones.

CDS, DVDS, AND GAMES

www.musicmagpie.co.uk
You can use this store when you are clearing out your CD and DVD collection. Just fill in the barcode of CDs, DVDs, or games to get an immediate price. Using the freepost service, you can download and print labels. Attach these to a box and drop off at your local post office. If sending over 50 items, you can use their courier service for a home pick-up. Payment is by check (cheque), e-voucher or charitable donation on receipt of goods.

PHOTOGRAPHIC EQUIPMENT

www.mpbphotographic.co.uk
This site will purchase all Canon and Nikon professional digital SLR photographic equipment as well as digital accessories from other manufacturers. They also purchase compact system cameras and lenses from Panasonic, Olympus, and Sony. Fill in a form for a quotation. Cameras can be posted or picked up by courier. Payment, once cameras are checked over, is by the BACS system.

www.realcamera.co.uk
Sevendale House, 7 Dale Street, Manchester M1 1JA.
0161 907 3236
This company buys any used photographic equipment of any type for reasonable prices. Call or visit the store for a quotation.

JEWELRY

www.cashforyourgold.co.uk
01902 623253
Check prices online for the weight of your gold jewelry. Then request an envelope and send off via Royal Mail special delivery. Payment is by cash or check (cheque).

www.gold2pounds.com
0800 3213003
Check prices online for the weight of your jewelry. Then request an insured freepost envelope and send your unwanted gold, silver, or platinum. Payment is by check (cheque) or money transfer.

www.postgoldforcash.com
0871 7168805
Check prices online for the weight of your gold jewelry. Then request a free gold-selling pack, list the gold, and send it in the envelope provided. Payment is by cash, bank transfer, or check (cheque).

CELL PHONES

www.envirofone.com
Check the price, and then provide your details. A padded envelope and freepost address label will be sent to you to post the phone back. Once the phone is tested and validated, you'll be sent an email confirming payment date.

www.mazumamobile.com
Search for your phone model online in the UK to get a price. Register your details, and a freepost bag will be sent to you. Post off your phone, and a check (cheque) will be sent to you on the day of receipt.

SPORTING EQUIPMENT

www.playitagainsports.com
Call your nearest Playitagain sports store in the US to find out the most asked-for items. Make sure your items are clean, in good condition, and include all necessary parts. Bring them to your local store for trade and payment on the spot.

ONLINE AUCTION STORES

www.ebay.co.uk
This is still the main international online auction site, where you can sell anything. Before you put up your items for sale, research similar goods already offered on the site for a description and price comparison. You have to include a digital photo of your item, and remember to include all post and packing in the cost. Follow instructions to create a seller's account, invoice your buyer, and once payment is received, send off the goods.

SECONDHAND STORES

www.cashgenerator.co.uk
Check online for your local store in the UK. Cash Generator will buy secondhand musical instruments and sports and electronic equipment. The most wanted items are laptops, phones, cameras, musical instruments, and games consoles. You get paid in cash from an agreed valuation.

CAR BOOT SALES

These happen regularly throughout the UK and the US and are normally advertised by flyers or in local newspapers. Do your research on e-bay to get an idea of price for any items of value. You generally have to arrive quite early in the morning to get a good pitch. Make sure all your items are clean and in good condition. Put similar pieces together and decide on your prices. Label each item with a clear price tag—most people are seeking bargains. Display everything on tables. Display the most saleable items where they can be seen best and picked up by potential buyers. Junk and toys can be laid out on a sheet on the ground. Clothes are a big seller, so display them well on a clothes rail. Take plenty of small change and have some plastic bags for customers who need them.

GARAGE/YARD/HOUSE SALES

Set a date and time for the sale and advertise in a local newspaper. State clearly what you are selling. For clothes and footwear, specify sizes and capitalize on the season. Popular items include sports cards, lawn mowers, camping articles, old books, jewelry, toys, and furniture. Set up tables to display the merchandise and price everything. If you live in a block, you may want to get together with some of your neighbors to hold a sale.

donating

THRIFT OR CHARITY STORES

The Thrift Shopper
www.thethriftshopper.com
In the US, look at this website to find details of your local thrift store.

In the UK, many high-street charity stores will take secondhand items. You can find your nearest store online. Websites for a few of the main charities are listed opposite. Most shops will accept good-quality, clean clothing, shoes and boots, jewelry, bags, and accessories.

When you have worked through the household section of this book, bear in mind they also accept books, CDs, DVDs, vinyl, musical instruments, homewares, soft furnishings, toys and games, stamps, and coins. They may not accept electronic equipment. Furniture can normally be picked up by arrangement.

Cancer Research UK
http://cancerresearchuk.org

Oxfam
www.oxfam.org.uk

British Heart Foundation
www.bhf.org.uk

Barnardo's
www.barnardos.org.uk

Marie Curie Cancer Care
www.mariecurie.org.uk

British Red Cross
www.redcross.org.uk

Housing Works
www.housingworks.org

Deseret Industries
www.deseretindustries.org

Goodwill
www.goodwill.org

Salvation Army
www.salvationarmy.org.uk

PART 3

clearing out the home

Hoarding household clutter takes a lot of maintenance and creates dust. Having junk all over the place has a bad effect on everyone living in your home. It slows down the energy, the chi, which is the life force of everything, creating a dull, fusty atmosphere that makes it feel like everyone is walking through treacle. By going through the rooms in your home and clearing out more of the possessions that you don't need or use any more, you will notice a lighter, brighter, happier ambience, which will permeate every family member. After your massive clear-out, you can start to enjoy the emotional and spiritual freedom that having fewer possessions to deal with brings.

lose that household clutter

You must be feeling very pleased with yourself if you have worked your way through the 100-item challenge and have reached your goal of just 100 belongings. But don't feel you can give up yet! Now you are in the frame of mind to let go of stuff, have a look at all the other family or shared household items in all the rooms of your home. The chances are it would be good to release some of these in line with the more minimalist ideas you are adopting. To see how much clutter you have acquired, look around each room with a dispassionate eye. Check all the shelves and cabinets to decide what you want, and need, and what you feel you can lose.

The entry hall or porch are the first places that may stop you in your tracks. It is so easy just to dump things in this area. Gradually, over time, everyone gets used to the junk and just squeezes past, or steps over it, every time they come in. You may also be surprised at what you find at the back of those units in the living room; perhaps craft projects that never got finished have been stored there, or maybe a pile of old DVDs has been pushed in there and forgotten. Books may be your problem. An extensive collection can seem great, but if you never read them and they are just gathering dust, they become superfluous to your needs. The kitchen can be another real eye-opener. You may be astonished to find a yogurt-maker or bread-maker, which seemed such a good idea at the time, hidden at the back of a cabinet. You may have used it once and now it's just taking up space. Or you may discover that you have three sets of dinner plates but only regularly use one set. And how many mugs do you actually use?

CLUTTERED ROOMS

Bedrooms can be the worst rooms in the house. I have been amazed at how cluttered clients' bedrooms are—a lot of them are certainly not the peaceful havens they should be. Look under your beds: drawers that are storing bedlinen are fine but if this area is full of old junk, you are not going to have restful sleep. Children's bedrooms today often have good storage systems to hold all the toys and games, but if these are full of discarded play things, it does not create a good, positive atmosphere. It can be hard to clear out children's bedrooms, so you will have to enlist their help, encouraging them to donate any of their unwanted or unused toys to more needy children.

Your bathroom may be a shock, too. Perhaps it's cluttered with half-finished bottles of shampoo, conditioner, or other products that you are no longer using. They may be lingering in the bathroom cabinet or stacked around the bath. Try to picture how much better it will look when it is clutter-free.

Excess paperwork, old files, magazines, and brochures are the main problem in the home office, so make sure you have a paper shredder on hand for when you start to turn this space into a creative and inspiring retreat.

In many homes, the attic is the dumping ground, hanging over you like a black cloud, and you may well feel reluctant to venture inside it. However, take a quick look to see the extent of the clear-out needed. You may be amazed by how much stuff has ended up there.

WHAT IS DEFINED AS CLUTTER?

Clutter is any household item, or any other possession, that you no longer like or use. It can be an unwanted present, or something that is broken and that you will never repair.

As mentioned earlier in the book, emotional attachment to possessions is a human weakness. The fact that a close relative or friend has given you something makes it harder to relinquish, even if you don't really like it. But that works against you because if you keep too many old possessions, they will keep you stuck in the past and not allow entry to all the exciting new opportunities or events that are waiting to come in. Your home is supposed to mirror you, so if it is cluttered and messy, you will be running your life in a very disorganized way.

ASSESSING YOUR CLUTTER

Now that you have looked at the scale of the task, you need to make a more detailed assessment in order to decide which cluttered areas to start clearing out first. Take a large writing pad and pen and go around each room, noting down where the main piles of junk are located. Mark whether they are in a unit, in a closet, on shelves, or just piled on the floor, and whether big or small. Use a highlighter pen to mark the piles and the room that irritate you the most, and make a start there. Have plenty of heavy-duty trash bags ready for all the items you no longer need.

Remember, it can be very emotional letting go of possessions you have had for years, so take it slowly, working on a room for a few hours at a time. It's much better to declutter when you are in a positive frame of mind.

how clutter affects your home

In the ancient Chinese art of feng shui, good energy (chi) flow through the home is essential for harmonious living. Chi is the invisible, subtle electromagnetic energy that flows everywhere, and within everything, bringing life force with it. In the West, there are no specific words relating to chi. We tend to use words such as "mood," "atmosphere," or "spirit" of ` a room or home to describe our feelings when we sense it. As a feng shui consultant, my aim is to manipulate and balance this energy to create a bright and uplifting feel in the home.

Chi enters through the front door and moves in a circular, snakelike fashion through the home, exiting through the back door or windows, where more chi enters and leaves through the front door. Chi needs a positive passage through the home, so if it encounters any piles of clutter or other blockages, it slows down, making it sluggish and lethargic.

One of the worst places to have piles of clutter is in your entry hall or by the front door. This is because you are blocking the "mouth" of the home where chi first enters. If chi meets clutter here, and elsewhere, it struggles to move around the home, which can be detrimental to the family or people living there. People can feel confused, indecisive, or just stuck in a rut. When you surround yourself with possessions that you love and use on a regular basis, they give out a positive, vibrant energy that encourages normal chi flow and produces an atmosphere that makes you feel happy and content. Loved, wanted, and used items support and nurture you through invisible connecting strands. But if your home is full of unwanted junk or broken items, their negative vibes will only pull you down. The problem, too, is that the longer the junk stays around, the worse its effects on you will be. By getting rid of unwanted possessions, you will lighten your load and immediately feel better mentally, physically, and spiritually.

CLUTTER BLACKSPOTS

There are several major areas in the home where clutter can gather and affect how you are living, and your progress in life:

Entry hall and porch

If this area is crowded with children's paraphernalia, shoes, bags, boxes, flyers, umbrellas, and junk mail, the chi can get blocked. This can result in life becoming a struggle, with some new opportunities and prospects barred.

Understairs cupboard

It is very easy to overload this space with old sports equipment, boxes of junk, tools, electrical appliances, or old cans of paint. This in turn creates a stagnant atmosphere that will filter up to the next floor where you sleep, making life seem like hard work.

Desk

If your home-office desk is full of paperwork, old files, reports, unused reference books, magazines, and Post-it notes, it can encourage confusion, making you feel out of control.

Attic

Unfortunately, these are often the dumping grounds for our past. Too many mementoes from childhood are stored here. Broken or disused furniture, electrical items, old toys, or other unwanted pieces end up here, too, making you feel over-burdened.

Bathroom

If you have half-finished beauty or bathing products stacked around the bath and are not likely to use them up, and units full of old medical supplies and unused samples, this private retreat will make you feel restless and unsettled.

is general or family clutter taking over your life?

This questionnaire will help you realize where you have a problem with household clutter, now that you have got to grips with your personal possessions. Score 2 points for a "Yes," 1 for a "Sometimes," and zero for a "No."

	Yes	Sometimes	No

general

1 Are you upset by the household clutter in your home but can't seem to make a start on getting rid of it?

2 Is your home full of inherited furniture that you don't really like?

3 Have you got unwanted electrical items or gadgets that you just don't use?

4 Does a family member have problems throwing things away?

5 Is your garage full of junk because there is no room in the attic?

6 Do you still have boxes from your last move that have never been opened?

entry hall

7 Is this full of old umbrellas, junk mail, discarded shoes, magazines, and newspapers that never get recycled?

kitchen

8 Have you got appliances hidden away that are never used?

9 Are there several sets of china in your cabinets, but just one that you use regularly?

10 Do you have double the amount of mugs ever used?

living room

11 Are there racks full of old DVDs, CDs, and games hardly played?

12 Do you have stacks of candles that you never seem to get around to using?

bedroom

13 Do you tend to store all your discarded or broken items under the bed?

14 Have you placed boxes of things you don't use on top of the closet just to get them out of the way?

bathroom

15 Is your bathroom overstocked with beauty or bath products that will never be used?

16 Are frayed and torn towels stacked in your bathroom cabinet?

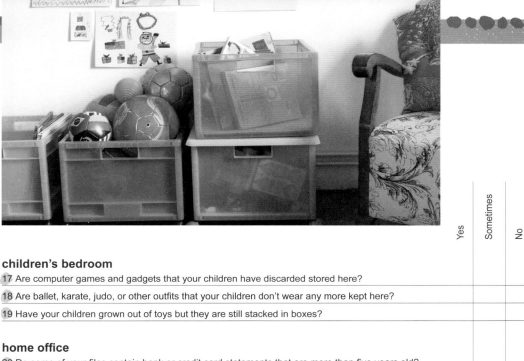

	Yes	Sometimes	No
children's bedroom			
17 Are computer games and gadgets that your children have discarded stored here?			
18 Are ballet, karate, judo, or other outfits that your children don't wear any more kept here?			
19 Have your children grown out of toys but they are still stacked in boxes?			
home office			
20 Do some of your files contain bank or credit card statements that are more than five years old?			
21 Have you old computers, printers, or other equipment stacked in a corner?			
22 Are your filing cabinets bulging with papers not cleared out in the last year?			
attic			
23 Do you actually know what you have stored in your attic?			
24 Can you easily get into your attic and is everything tidily stored and labeled?			
25 Do you almost have enough goods in the attic to set up a new home?			
TOTAL			

the results

40–50 You have a problem with household clutter and it is depleting your energy levels, so now is the time to start to let go. Work through the rooms one at a time, taking the advice on the following pages, clearing out what is no longer wanted or needed. You are on your journey to a junk-free life.

30–39 Household clutter is building up in your home and detrimentally affecting the moods of everyone living there. Go through your home gradually, clearing out superfluous items, and see how good it makes you feel.

20–39 Clutter is starting to appear in your home, so get to grips with it now, removing what is not needed, and see how the overall atmosphere improves.

Below 20 Clutter is not an issue for you, but keep a close eye on what you buy. Ask yourself, "Do I need it? Is it really useful to my life?"

doorway and entry hall

This is one of the most important parts of the home to keep clutter-free because in feng shui terms it is the "mouth" of the home where chi first enters, which makes it vital to keep the area as vibrant and clean and tidy as possible. The doorway and hall should be bright and welcoming to all your visitors. If they can hardly get through the door because of all the junk that has accumulated behind it, they will feel irritated right from the start of their visit.

An overcrowded hall will get you down as well. If you constantly have to climb over a mountain of stuff just to get to the kitchen, you will feel exhausted before you even make the coffee you have been longing for. Before you start your clear-out, try to envision your ideal, streamlined, clutter-free hall. Really think how you would like it to be: Do you see it newly painted with a useful storage cabinet or maybe a table with drawers? Or perhaps you see it with polished floorboards and a striking coat stand?

GETTING STARTED
time to spend on clear-out: 2 hours

To start on your hall, get your garbage bags together, labeling one "things to sell," another "junk," and a third one "recycling." Separately label large items that won't fit in the bags. Work efficiently for the time allocated, going through the Clutter Culprits (see below) and their solutions, adding any other things that you have accumulated. If this area is really cluttered and you can't get through it all in one session, allow another one to tackle what is left. This area will seem much more spacious when it's junk-free, and the atmosphere will become bright and inspiring, helping you to move on in life.

CLUTTER CULPRITS

All manner of items gather in hallways. Use these solutions to sort them out.

Problem: piles of shoes, boots, sneakers, bags
Solution: dispose of worn-out shoes or bags. Install a slim-line, pull-out unit that can hold several pairs of shoes. Make sure everyone takes their workbags to their rooms.

Problem: junk mail, flyers, leaflets, old bills, unopened credit card bills and charity collection envelopes, take-out menus, taxi or tradespeople cards, old newspapers, old keys
Solution: recycle unwanted leaflets and paper. Pay outstanding bills and file the rest. Keep wanted menus and cards in a file with plastic inserts. Dispose of old, unused keys.

Problem: bicycles, strollers (pushchairs), golf clubs, rackets, discarded sports gear
Solution: sell anything that is not used any more. Store bicycles, strollers, and sports equipment outdoors or, if appropriate, on wall-mounted brackets or under the stairs.

Problem: home repair (DIY) materials, old tools, paints, and other paraphernalia under the stairs
Solution: safely dispose of any old tools, paints, glue, or fillers. Put up shelving or hooks to store wanted equipment.

living room

This is your room for relaxation. It is often the focal point of the home, and a place where you can recover and unwind with your family or friends after a hard day's work. Multifunctional living often exists here: there may be a space for dining and also a corner for a home office, from which the household is run efficiently.

Having a good furniture layout with sofas and chairs grouped around a central coffee table encourages people to relax, enjoying each other's company and the conviviality. But if this room is full of clutter and too much furniture, it gives off a restless and disturbing atmosphere, making everyone feel reluctant to linger for long in the space. No one wants to be surrounded by clutter in this room; it just makes you feel frustrated and annoyed in what should be a calm, pleasant room.

Bearing in mind your mission to live with fewer possessions, picture in your head the ideal layout for your junk-free living space. Do you see it with good storage units? Maybe you visualize it with less furniture and the shelves cleared of some of your accessories and books for a cleaner, tidier look? Perhaps you see yourself throwing out your two old sofas and replacing them with a big corner sofa?

finding joy

Planning a more spacious and organized layout will spur you on to clear out the clutter and achieve a living space you can really enjoy.

Problem: old magazines
Solution: cut out any articles of interest to keep for reference and file in a plastic-sleeved folder, and recycle the rest.

Problem: too many accessories
Solution: if you are fed up with a lot of the objects on your shelves, decide which ones you still love and take the rest to a thrift (charity) store, or sell them at a car boot or garage sale.

Problem: damaged or broken furniture
Solution: take to the dump any pieces that cannot be repaired or you don't like any more. Alternatively, arrange a collection from a thrift (charity) store. If you still want to keep the piece, have it repaired by professionals.

Problem: inherited items, such as relatives' knickknacks, clocks, pictures, ceramic collections
Solution: keep only what you really love and items that will always remind you of the person who owned them originally. Dispose of any mementoes that are worthless, and sell good clocks, pictures, or collections at auction or to an antique store.

CLUTTER CULPRITS
Follow these solutions to achieve some order once more in this room.

Problem: overloaded bookshelves
Solution: keep the books you love and take all those unwanted ones to a thrift (charity) store, or donate them to a hospital or school library.

Problem: old CDs, DVDs, games
Solution: sort out the ones that are not played anymore and sell them on through specialist or secondhand stores, or online. Alternatively, take them to a thrift (charity) store.

Problem: loose photographs and old albums
Solution: go through these when you are feeling strong—photographs can make you very emotional. Throw out unwanted shots or pictures of people you can't remember, no longer see, or dislike. Think about storing photos in index systems, so it's easy to leaf through them. Look through your old albums and try to refine them—if you have eight, for example, try to cut them down to four, including the photos you love.

GETTING STARTED
time to spend on clear-out: 4 hours

Collect some garbage bags. Label the first bag "things to sell," the next one "junk," and the third one "friends or thrift/charity." Put labels on large items. Sort steadily through the Clutter Culprits on the left, plus anything else that may not be included on the list. If your living room is really overloaded and you can't get through it all in one session, allow time for another one. Once you have cleared out all the unwanted items, your living room will start to breathe again, and you will love its positive, vibrant atmosphere, which will make you want to invite friends over.

my journal

I'm rushing to write this, because I'm going out to dinner tonight. At least I can easily find what I want to wear in my pared-down wardrobe. Do I miss what's gone? I don't think so—I am virtually down to my 100 items, so that's good. What is really tough is not browsing around the stores as much as I used to, because I know I may be tempted to buy something I don't desperately need. I avoided the sales like the plague but okay, "hands-up," I did buy some much-needed pantyhose and socks but, honestly, they were replacing ones that have worn out.

Moving on… I ventured into the kitchen the other day with my de-cluttering hat on. I didn't think I was that bad with household items but

I have lived in this house for several years now and many things have still not seen the light of day. What do you think? Do you keep baking equipment you only use once or twice a year? I don't know about you but some dishes I use all the time and others just seem to sit there. I kept a set of cups for visitors but have only used mugs since I moved. And 27 cookbooks! How did I end up with so many? And I have used just a few recipes from each one—okay, I can feel a purge coming on.

kitchen

A warm and nurturing environment, the kitchen is often thought of as the "heart" of the home. It's the place where people come together to enjoy food and catch up with each other.

The ideal kitchen has clear, tidy countertops, adequate storage, and ordered cabinets, making this room an uplifting place to be. However, countertops are often cluttered with every gadget imaginable, cabinets are overflowing with china and kitchen products, and fridges and freezers contain food that will never get eaten. This overcrowding can upset the balance and harmony needed here. Friends and family will get fed up searching for that buried egg whisk or trying to find that packet of white sauce in a cabinet—somewhere.

Before you get to grips with de-junking your kitchen and having a simpler lifestyle, think what your ideal kitchen would be like. Do you see tidy cabinets with some pull-out baskets and products neatly ordered? Have you a vision of gleaming, clear countertops and a floor with nothing stacked on it?

CLUTTER CULPRITS

Take note of these solutions to achieve a workable streamlined space.

Problem: unused or broken china, duplicate dinner or tea sets, old mugs and casserole dishes
Solution: throw out broken china. Take old dishes, mugs, and dinner or tea sets to a thrift (charity) store, or sell online or through a newspaper.

Problem: unwanted gadgets, such as yogurt or ice-cream makers and juicers
Solution: if these are working and in good condition, sell them online or through a local newspaper. Alternatively, give them to friends.

Problem: too many packaged kitchen products, sauces, cans, oils, and spices
Solution: throw out what's stale; give away what's not needed. Store similar items together. Use baskets to create some tidy storage in cabinets.

Problem: decaying cleaning products
Solution: throw out old cleaning liquids (dispose of them responsibly) and cleaning cloths; keep only what you use regularly, and store in pull-out baskets. Give away any unwanted, impulse buys that you find.

GETTING STARTED
time to spend on clear-out: 3 hours

Collect your garbage bags. Label one "things to sell" (use a box for big gadgets), label the second "junk," and the third "friends or thrift (charity) store." Go through the Clutter Culprits list above, adding anything else you may have. Schedule in another session if you need more time. Cleared cabinets and countertops will make preparation and cooking a pleasure again, and the uplifting atmosphere will attract people like a magnet.

bedroom

Your bedroom is your personal sanctuary, a place where you can close the door behind you and escape work or home worries. Winding down in bed, you can calm your mind, emotions, and spirit in this soothing, peaceful space. You can also escape here for a nap after a tiring day or to grab some time just for yourself, to read on your own.

Since this is a place where your body re-generates itself and your spirit rests, you want to be soothed and pampered by the atmosphere. The clean lines of a comfortable bed with coordinated bedding positioned opposite the door, balanced by bedside cabinets and lamps, a tidy wardrobe or closet, and a dressing table, will make you sigh with pleasure as you enter the room. Boxes toppling off the top of the closet, clothes dumped on the floor, an overflowing laundry hamper, and junk thrown under the bed will generate a completely opposite response: your heart will sink every time you enter this untidy, muddled room.

A clutter-free bedroom is essential for good sleep, and should be a priority in your quest for a simpler life. How do you want this room to be? Do you see a room painted in pleasant pastel colors with a cozy bed, complementary bedlinen, and big, plumped-up pillows? Perhaps you want a more feminine look with frilly drapes and lacy bed coverings, or maybe you would like the bed to be tented? Alternatively, a more modern room with contrasting, neutral color shades may be the style you want?

GETTING STARTED
time to spend on clear-out: 2–3 hours

Collect your garbage bags. Label the first "junk," the second "friends or thrift (charity) store." Work positively through the Clutter Culprits list on the right, adding anything extra you have stashed here. If you find yourself battling to get everything done in the time specified, just allocate time for another clear-out. As the clutter disappears, you will feel a positive shift in atmosphere. The "fug" will lift and your bedroom will be a safe haven once more.

Aim to make your bedroom an uncluttered, peaceful space that helps you to start and end each day feeling relaxed and with a clear mind.

CLUTTER CULPRITS

Use the solutions to tidy up the room.

Problem: boxes of junk on top of the closets
Solution: these will give you a headache, because you will think they are going to fall on you so sort through the boxes and throw out what's not needed. Store the remainder in pull-out boxes or baskets inside cabinets.

Problem: a pile of broken hair dryers, old shoes, old bedlinen, discarded T-shirts under the bed
Solution: safely dispose of the hair dryers and other broken electrical equipment. Throw out old shoes, bedlinen, and T-shirts. Any in good condition, take to a thrift (charity) store. For more storage, have drawers under the bed but only store clean, untorn bedlinen or extra clothes here.

child's bedroom

Many children consider their bedrooms to be their special place, where they can hide from the world, play games, read, make up wonderful stories, work on their computer, listen to music, and entertain their friends. It can often be a dual-purpose room with a quiet area for relaxing and sleeping and another, more stimulating space for playing and studying.

An ordered desk, a comfy bed with colorful bedlinen, and toys stored away in stacking boxes will make your child feel safe and secure. But, as we know, children can be notoriously untidy, and will often leave toys, books, and clothes scattered around the room. Their work or play area can be a disaster of discarded cars, dolls, electronic games, computer games, old paintings, and schoolwork. All this confusion can make the energy restless here, disturbing children's schoolwork and upsetting their sleep.

Before you start working on your child's bedroom clutter, try to visualize this room when it is de-junked. Are you encouraging your child to follow your simple living ethos? Do you see a desk in the corner with shelves above it stacked with loved books, disks, and games? Do you imagine the bed with a supportive headboard and soft lamps on tables either side of the bed? Have all the remaining toys and games miraculously been stored in big colorful drawers or in stacking boxes? Perhaps soft toys, if your child is young, are now hanging in canvas hanging racks with numerous pockets?

GETTING STARTED
time to spend on clear-out: 2 hours

Work on this room together with your child. Collect your garbage bags. Label one "junk," another "toys to sell," and a third "thrift (charity) store." Label a large box for bigger toys, or just label them separately. Go through the Clutter Culprits list on the right and if the room is too overloaded to get through it all in one session, just book in another one. After a few arguments, your child will sigh with relief as his/her special room emerges from its clutter, making him/her feel nurtured and happy once more.

CLUTTER CULPRITS

Use the solutions to restore order.

Problem: piles of toys and games
Solution: throw away anything that is broken.
Give toys in good condition to thrift (charity)
stores or hospitals, or to sales held to raise
money for your child's school.

Problem: too many computer and electronic
games, old CDs and DVDs
Solution: give to friends, sell via online sites,
such as e-bay, or to secondhand stores, or
donate to sales for your child's school.

Problems: stacks of books
Solution: keep the well-loved favorites and give
away the rest to charities or other good causes.

Problem: unwanted or outgrown clothes
Solution: check what clothes your child likes to
wear and pass on unwanted or outgrown items
to children of friends or hold an exchange party.
Alternatively, take them to a thrift (charity) store.

bathroom

Sinking into a hot, fragrant bath is one of life's pleasures. Relaxing in the calming water, you can wash away any negativity from the day and forget your problems, cleansing your mind, body, and soul. Here you can escape from the demands of your family and the outside world, and have some time for contemplation or meditation.

What you need in this space is a warm and appealing atmosphere; it should be a place to linger, where you will feel cherished. Being surrounded by fluffy towels and mats, calming pictures, and tidy storage cabinets and hanging units can make you feel that you are in your own unique retreat. Surfaces packed full of half-finished bathing and beauty products, too many units or baskets, and fraying or torn towels bring out exactly the opposite response: you just feel restless, dissatisfied, and unsettled in this messy room.

An inviting, organized bathroom will help you chill and take time out, and is a must for the "life with less" that you are seeking. But how do you see the refuge of your dreams? Has it got cabinets with tidily stacked products, or maybe units with pull-out drawers so that you can find things easily? Maybe your ideal is a freestanding unit with open shelves so that you can store your towels? Is the bath tub cleared of all clogged-up products and surrounded by candles?

CLUTTER CULPRITS

Use the following solutions to bring some order to the bathroom.

Problem: full medicine cabinet
Solution: throw away out-of-date creams, plasters, and ointments. Return antibiotics or other strong pills to the pharmacy to be disposed of responsibly.

Problem: too many bath oils, shampoos, conditioners, and other beauty products, often half-finished
Solution: throw away opened products that you will never use again and that are cluttering up the bath and shower. Give away any that are unopened. Hang up a new cabinet or buy a unit, if necessary, and store what you want to keep, tidily, so you can find what you need.

Problem: old towels and mats, and units cluttering up the bathroom
Solution: dispose of torn, worn, or stained towels and mats—they just pull down the energy here. Store the ones you've kept by color in a unit. Sell any unwanted units locally.

GETTING STARTED
time to spend on clear-out: 1½–2 hours

Collect your garbage bags. Label the first one "junk." If you have pieces of furniture to dispose of, just put a label on them. Label a second bag "friends or thrift (charity) store." Make sure you go through the Clutter Culprits list above, adding anything not included there. Two hours should be enough time but add on a bit more if you are still not finished. Once this room is cleared of all the garbage, notice how "light" and inviting it seems once more.

home office

A creative and inspiring environment, this is where you spend time paying bills, juggling the household budget, and possibly doing your own freelance work. Clarity and concentration are important here in order for you to make the right decisions. If you are doing your own work in this space, it is here that you promote yourself to the world, showing your talent for bringing wealth, prosperity, and success into your life.

For you to achieve this, the room should be pleasant, well lit, and organized, with all the equipment you need at your fingertips. However, your creativity and positive attitude will slide if your desk is covered with paperwork, bills, Post-its, pens, and crumpled stationery. If you are surrounded by gadgets that no longer work, and filing cabinets that you can hardly open, your heart will sink every time you enter this workroom.

An ordered office will boost your business skills, and help you plan how to spend less money in your simplified lifestyle. So how do you see this productive area working? Do you see a bright room with an attractive wooden filing cabinet, tidy desk, and stacking filing trays for all your bills and correspondence? Or if your office is in your living room, does it contain an ingenious unit that folds away but contains slimline drawers and a sliding flap for typing on your laptop?

GETTING STARTED
time to spend on clear-out: 2 hours

Collect some trash bags. Label the first one "recycling," the second "junk," and a third "thrift (charity) store." If you have equipment or furniture to dispose of, label it separately. Follow your Clutter Culprits list on the right, including anything else that is not listed there. If your office is packed with paperwork or old equipment, schedule in some more time to finish clearing out. When order is restored to this creative room, and the "mustiness" and untidiness disappear, you will notice how inspired and mentally alert you feel sitting at your desk.

CLUTTER CULPRITS

Use these solutions to take control of this creative space once more.

Problem: messy desk
Solution: shred any old correspondence that's not needed. File any bills or important letters. Transfer numbers, notes, or addresses on Post-its to your phone or diary. Junk any old stationery, leaking pens, or broken pencils.

Problem: packed filing cabinet
Solution: sort through your files, recycling where possible and shredding anything else that is redundant until you have a neat, workable, and current cabinet.

Problem: old furniture, broken or unused electrical equipment
Solution: remove unwanted furniture and donate to a thrift (charity) store if appropriate (arrange collection for large pieces). Dump broken equipment at your local refuse facility, sell unused pieces online or at a secondhand store.

attic

How do you view your attic? Do you see it as a space to dump unused things, or to store relics from your past? The attic all too often becomes a junkyard for our memories, stockpiling inherited items that no one wants, old school trophies and awards, discarded toys, romantic memorabilia, and unwanted sports equipment.

Your home's past seems to linger here, hanging over your family and friends like a murky, dark cloud. Unwanted gifts can be abandoned into this dark space, leaving a feeling of negativity and disapproval. An attic can be a perfect, well-lit space, with good storage units, where you can keep rarely used possessions. But if you can hardly get into it because of the boxes packed to the roof, or the mass of junk that has been dumped there, you will feel chained to your past and scared of moving forward.

A tidy, well-organized, and junk-free attic will take you well on your path to living with less. But what does your ideal attic space look like? Has it got good shelving, clearly labeled boxes, hanging rails for sports clothes, and units for tools? Do you see it brightly lit with everything neatly sorted on racks?

GETTING STARTED
time to spend on clear-out: 3-4 hours

Collect some garbage bags. Label the first one "junk" (you may need several), the second "recycling," the third "thrift (charity) store," and the fourth "things to sell." Go through your Clutter Culprits list (see opposite), adding any items not detailed there. A packed attic may take more than four hours to sort out, so book another session. Clearing out old junk from your past and tidying up the attic will bring a huge shift in energy.

finding joy

Clear your attic and the heavy "cloud" above you will lift, giving you the impetus to move forward once again.

CLUTTER CULPRITS

Follow the solutions to reclaim your storage space.

Problem: old equipment, such as exercise bikes, golf clubs, old skis, rackets, and mini trampolines
Solution: throw out any decrepit equipment, sell anything in good condition online or to a secondhand store, or give it to a good cause.

Problem: memorabilia, such as old schoolbooks, college and school projects, diplomas or degrees, love letters
Solution: keep diplomas, have a special "memories" box for a few love letters and treasured items, and ditch the rest.

Problem: old games and playing cards, old toys
Solution: keep any games and playing cards that you will play again regularly and give away the rest.

Problem: old decorating materials
Solution: throw out opened paints, stains, or varnishes that are no longer usable, dried-up brushes, and old rags. Keep recently used paint (for touching up), and cleaned brushes, rollers, and trays in a labeled plastic storage container.

back yard (garden)

This is your retreat from the world, a place where you can relax and sunbathe or read a book on a summer's afternoon. It is here that you grow beautiful, scented flowers or harvest bountiful produce for everyone to enjoy. On balmy afternoons and evenings, you can entertain your friends and family with barbecues or light, summer meals, relishing the long, daylight hours.

Manicured lawns, a spotless patio or decked area, and glorious shrubs will feed your soul every time you walk into this type of garden. But if you have to pick your way over the cracked or moss-laden patio onto the overgrown lawn, being attacked by prickly bushes every step of the way, you will feel annoyed, irritated, and let down by this neglected and forgotten area.

A well-laid-out and organized garden will help keep you in the right frame of mind for a less stressful lifestyle. But how do you see your dream garden? Does it have a tidy lawn, a pergola, and a host of colorful flowers? Or do you prefer a raised patio area for eating and then a paved garden with lots of colorful pots and summer blooms?

GETTING STARTED
time to spend on clear-out: 3 hours

Use several heavy-duty garden trash bags. Add a garbage bag labeled "things to sell" and another labeled "thrift (charity) store." Work down the Clutter Culprits list (see opposite), adding any bits and pieces not included. If you find that three hours is not long enough to tame your back yard (garden), arrange time for another session. Restoring your back yard to its former glory will remove the air of decay. You will be able to smell the flowers, and be tempted to linger here, enjoying your outside space once more.

CLUTTER CULPRITS

Use the solutions to make your back yard (garden) more appealing.

Problem: faded, broken, or unused garden furniture; ripped or stained cushions
Solution: ditch any furniture that is irreparable. Otherwise, repair broken wooden supports, restain and revarnish where appropriate, and replace fabric or cushions. Sell or give away unwanted furniture in good condition.

Problem: shed or garden building full of rusting tools, old or unused machinery, decaying barbecues, broken bicycles, and old plant fertilizers
Solution: junk any old equipment and bicycles, old plant foods, seeds, and any gadgets that are beyond repair. Sort out what machinery and

tools you want to keep, and clean and oil them. Hang cleaned tools on hooks or a tool bar. Sell the rest. Add more shelves to take equipment off the floor. Store often-used chairs and barbecues by the door.

Problem: decaying, cracked, or chipped flowerpots, and pots full of weeds
Solution: throw out frost-damaged pots or any beyond repair. Clean up and re-use the others. Fill with new potting soil and grow some seasonal flowering plants to boost the energy here.

PART 4

your new minimalist life

Living a simpler life with fewer possessions in your home can be totally liberating. Releasing things you have kept for a while brings in a new, fresh energy that affects everybody. With clearer surroundings comes a clearer mind and more time to focus on things that matter to you. Perhaps you can take time to set some more spiritual goals. What is it that your inner self, your heart, really desires for the next few years?

living a simpler lifestyle

How has getting rid of your clutter gone? Are you close to living with just 100 items? I expect it has been quite an emotional journey. Letting go of once-loved belongings is never easy, but as soon as they are gone, you can feel truly free. Do you look around your home now and feel that every painting, every accessory, and every book means something special to you? You may find that once you start releasing household items, you can't stop.

You can appreciate the open spaces in your home. You no longer keep tripping over things, and it gives you a wonderful, free feeling. Your life is less stressful and more contemplative. Some people decide to live with very little furniture and soft furnishings; others decide they need more to achieve the level of comfort they want. Just go with what feels right for you.

Becoming more of a minimalist does not mean that you can't own things. We all need a certain level of material comfort. It just means that you have stepped away from excessive consumerism on your way to a more authentic life. Being more minimalist means promoting the things you value the most—decide what is really important in your life and remove those things that distract you from this. You can show your authentic self to the world, and take time to listen to your inner needs.

finding joy

Replace objects with experiences. Make a resolution to do all the things that you really love.

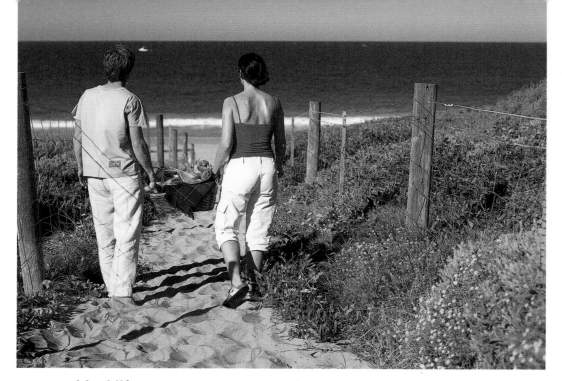

your ideal life

Allowing yourself some free time from "busy-ness," you can quieten that loud outer voice and connect with your inner whisperings about your future goals or dreams. As you build the image of your future, look around your home and see if the belongings you have left fit in with the image of your new life, or match your aspirations? Maybe you have always wanted to take up photography but have never found the time, and now you want to convert one of your bedrooms into a studio. Will you need to do some more clearing out to achieve this aim? Or perhaps you want to convert your garden shed or outbuilding into a small office so that you can simplify your life by working from home. Will you have to get rid of more tools and garden furniture that may be stored here? You may want to socialize more, and are longing to convert your garage into a spare guest room, but will you need to do a big clear-out first?

Clearing out your home allows for new thinking, and lets new opportunities present themselves. You may realize that you are ready for a more drastic change, possibly a move from the city to the country, for example. Working in an office may no longer appeal to you and you may decide to re-train as a therapist or work with animals.

living with less

Now that you have got used to living with less, you may feel you want to take it a stage further. Do you feel you still have too much furniture? One way of cutting down on furniture in the home is to exchange some items for multifunctional pieces. If you are using your spare room as an office, for example, and don't want a bed in there, think about having a sofa that converts into a bed in your living space. Perhaps replacing two sofas with one large one with a corner return would give you more space. Some single beds fold back into seats or side tables. Ingenious coffee tables can be converted into dining tables by adjusting the legs. Need more storage? Buy a chest that doubles up as a coffee table. To create more space in the center of your living room, buy a nest of tables, which can be stored by the wall and pulled out when needed. Some versatile shelf units have one side for books and accessories, and the other, narrower side for storing DVDs and games. If you have just got rid of some novels to the thrift (charity) store, think about buying an e-reader or join your local library.

If working in your living room is a necessity, consider a slimline desk with narrow drawers and a pull-out shelf for your laptop. Losing a storage unit in a bedroom? Units are available that slide under the bed. But only store clothes or bedlinen here, because a mix of other possessions can possibly disrupt your sleep.

When you remove excessive belongings from your life and step away from materialistic desires, it creates the opportunity for a significant life change to take place. When you get off the treadmill of a busy life, you need to stop for a moment and ask yourself, "What am I doing with my life? What will make me happy?" Think carefully about what you want out of your future, and take the necessary steps to achieve it.

finding joy

Living more simply can change you forever. You learn to "live in the now," appreciating every day of your wonderful existence.

my journal

I can't believe I have nearly finished writing the book—I have really been on a journey with it for the last few months. I am finding these dull winter days a bit depressing, but they do put me in the frame of mind to keep clearing out more stuff: I gave away two of my old summer baskets to a friend yesterday. I also decided that some chick-lit novels needed to go to the thrift (charity) store. I often buy them from the man on the beach, who sells a great selection, but they clutter up my shelves pretty quickly. Have I got the energy to tackle my office next? It's packed full of reference books that hardly seem to get looked at now… I have battled a bit with the challenge of living with 100 items but I have only replaced things since I started, and I have noticed a change in my shopping habits—I still lust after some pretty clothes but I make myself resist. How have you got on? I wish you well and hope you've made progress too, and will continue to enjoy living your life of less.

index

further reading

Babauta, Leo, *The Power of Less,* Hay House

James, Oliver, *Affluenza*, Ebury Publishing

Jay, Francine, *Joy of Less*, *A Minimalist Living Guide*, Anja Press

Lambert, Mary, *The Ultimate Guide to Clearing Your Clutter*, CICO Books

Luhrs, Janet, *Simple Living Guide*, Broadway

Oxenreider, Tsh, *Organized Simplicity*, Betterway Books

picture credits

acknowledgments

I would like to thank my managing editors, Dawn Bates and Clare Sayer, for their creative help in this project. A very special thank you goes to my sister Gill in Portugal, and to Simon, Emma, Marina, and Rafael in Italy, for all their support and encouragement when I was writing on those dark winter days. Finally, to my friends Claire M, Tim, Anna, Lucy, Liz, Claire G, Linda, Jackie, Sue, Fran, and Sarah, who dragged me away from my computer to have film nights and to go out for a few glasses of red wine and friendly conversation. Also thanks to Suzi, who always made me laugh over our fun lunches, and who gave me some useful input for my journal.

Mary Lambert is based in Shoreham-by-Sea and can be contacted for feng shui consultations for homes and businesses on mary.lambert8@gmail.com.